Meeting the One Who Loves You

Meeting the One *Who Loves You*

Saint Teresa of Ávila's Way of Prayer

By Shawn Chapman

Our Sunday Visitor
Huntington, Indiana

Nihil Obstat
Msgr. Michael Heintz, Ph.D.
Censor Librorum

Imprimatur
✠ Kevin C. Rhoades
Bishop of Fort Wayne-South Bend
March 28, 2025

The *Nihil Obstat* and *Imprimatur* are official declarations that a book is free from doctrinal or moral error. It is not implied that those who have granted the *Nihil Obstat* and *Imprimatur* agree with the contents, opinions, or statements expressed.

30 29 28 27 26 25 1 2 3 4 5 6 7 8 9

Our Sunday Visitor Publishing Division
Our Sunday Visitor, Inc.
200 Noll Plaza
Huntington, IN 46750
www.osv.com
1-800-348-2440

ISBN: 978-1-63966-288-3 (Inventory No. T2949)
1. RELIGION—Christian Living—Prayer.
2. RELIGION—Christianity—Saints & Sainthood.
3. RELIGION—Christianity—Catholic.

eISBN: 978-1-63966-289-0
LCCN: 2025937391

Cover and interior design: Chelsea Alt
Cover and interior art: Adobe Stock

PRINTED IN THE UNITED STATES OF AMERICA

For Zane Thibodeaux

Contents

Chapter One

St. Teresa of Jesus and the Prayer of Recollection

When Jesus turned and saw them following, he said to them,
"What are you looking for?" They said to him, "Rabbi"
(which means Master), "where are you staying?"
"Come," he replied, "and you will see."

— John 1:38–39

After reading a biography of St. Teresa of Ávila several years ago, I found myself powerfully drawn to her and her spirituality. I wanted to live it out in my own life the best I could, so I found a community of Secular Discalced Carmelites (the lay branch of her order) two hours away. I was excited. At my first meeting I felt that I had found a home among people who followed Jesus the way I wanted to follow him. Over time, I would come to know much more about this way — the way of Teresian prayer.

At that time, I was a few years widowed with small children. Every day was a fight for me just to do normal things that had to be done. Finding time for silent prayer on top of that seemed like a lot. Yet it turned out that learning to practice daily what Saint Teresa called "mental prayer" made my life easier because of the grace God brought me in it, especially the gift of peace.

When it came time for me to make a deeper commitment to my Carmelite community and my new way of life, however, I went through a painful period of confusion and doubt. Then one night, I felt Saint Teresa very close to me. I had the impression in the dark as I lay in my bed that she was stretched over me, that she covered me with her voluminous brown habit, arms open wide. This was so many years ago, but I remember it vividly. I understood that however confused, uncertain, or inadequate I felt about my new commitment, Teresa was claiming me.

The next day I was on a walk praying when a car sped by me, and someone threw a red rose out of the window. It landed at my feet in some sand that had gathered near the corner, and I heard an inner voice say, "I will plant this rose in the desert of Carmel."

I took this as a further confirmation that Teresa had claimed me and that I was called to this way of life.

Maybe God doesn't have to shake you or throw things at you to get through to you. Maybe he just put this book in your hands to call you to cast your net into the deep. Maybe all you need is someone who came to this prayer with a distracted mind and the busy life of a single mom to show you that anyone can pray Teresa's Prayer of Recollection (whether you're a part of the Carmelite order or not).

Wherever you are in life and in your walk with God, fear not. Only good can come of learning this prayer and making it an important part of your daily life. St. Teresa of Jesus knew the transforming love of God in prayer, and consequently, she lived a life of extraordinary richness. She left directions for us to try and see for ourselves how quietly powerful this prayer can be and how beautiful is the face of the Lord who lives within each of us.

Her guidance is truly for anyone, whatever your life circumstances may be. Come and you will see.

You can read this book from beginning to end before putting it into practice. Or you may find it more helpful and impactful as you get to Chapter Three, "Praying the Prayer of Recollection," to pause at the end of each section, put the book down, and practice what you just read for a moment before reading on.

Note: Throughout this book, all quotations are from Saint Teresa's writings, unless otherwise specified.

....

An Introduction to St. Teresa of Jesus

"I am yours. I was born for you. What do you want of me?"

— En los manos de Dios

In a sparse room with only a low, small bed for furniture, a nun is seated on the floor, scribbling without pause by the light of a small oil lamp. She writes on an accordion-folded and flattened sheaf of paper, which she has set on a corner ledge that serves as her desk. It's night. The other nuns are sleeping. She is tired and her head aches, but this is the only time she has to write lately, and write she must out of obedience to her confessor. But she is much inspired — watching her, one gets the sense she would write with both hands at once if she could.

So great are Saint Teresa's gifts of prayer and so inspired is her teaching that Catholic spirituality is indelibly stamped by it from this time forward. Through the centuries that follow, Christians who set out on what she calls the "Royal Road" of prayer will almost feel the brush of her rough brown habit from time to time. Though they be unknowing, she will pass by, leading the way to the Bridegroom with her lamp burning brightly.

Catholics during Teresa's lifetime (1515–1582) were deeply conflicted about interior prayer and mystical experience. Religious authorities were especially wary of women practicing mental prayer or experiencing mystical graces because they thought women were more easily influenced by the devil than men. Teresa wrote of this herself:

> Yet, Lord, I cannot believe this of thy goodness and righteousness, for thou art a righteous Judge, not like judges in the world, who, being, after all, men and sons of Adam, refuse to consider any woman's virtue as above suspicion. Yes, my King, but the day will come when all will be known. … When I see what the times are like, I feel it is not right to repel spirits which are virtuous and brave, even though they be the spirits of women.

Women at that time were not allowed to study theology or even the Bible. Certain books of the Bible were available in Spanish, but not many. Fr. Diego de Yanguas, one of Teresa's confessors, said that it was not right that a woman should write about Scripture and ordered Teresa's *Meditations on the Song of Songs* to be burned. We only have it today because of a secret copy made by a nun.

Even the first contemplative book Saint Teresa read, *The Third Spiritual Alphabet* by Francisco de Osuna, reflected the prevailing belief that mental prayer and theological reflection were not for women. The Inquisition held women contemplatives in high suspicion, and Saint Teresa had to go before them seven times both for her writings and the way she traveled about publicly. Women were not supposed to presume to teach, and it was socially unacceptable for them to go out unchaperoned. Ultimately, this cultural attitude toward women and contemplation helped form Teresa into the woman she was and led her to teach as she did. She would never have been able to do anything if she had not overcome those suspicions and prejudices within herself. She also learned to deal with them in the men around her who had power over the course of her life. Teresa had to experience a total transformation to navigate this and not let it stop her journey.

In addition to these prevailing views on women's spirituality, many people of Teresa's time were so fascinated by miracles and the supernatural that they thought these were the point of prayer, even the only true signs of holiness. Some insisted that meditating on the humanity of Jesus — or simply using his humanity as a springboard for the imagination in prayer — would be an obstacle to pure, imageless prayer, which they believed was the only true form of prayer.

The theologians of the time were almost always completely absorbed in the value of forms and rituals, doctrine and law, over lived experience and prayer.

There was also tension about the inner contemplative life of prayer and the "active life" of service in the world. Both sides thought they were on the surer and better path. It was common to pit Martha and Mary of Bethany against one another as if they were opposed.

Saint Teresa's ability to overcome these preconceptions of her time and culture is a testament to her unusual temerity, to her love of God, to the inner transformation she experienced in prayer, and to the truth of her calling. (To learn more specifically about Teresa in her cultural context, the book *Teresa of Jesus: Woman, Prophet, Mystic* from ICS Publications is ideal.)

In her writings on prayer, Teresa addressed these conflicts and concerns adroitly with her trademark, well-grounded wisdom. She struck a beautiful balance in her teachings. Mystical experiences that are from God, she argued, bestow grace on the soul and can be known by their fruits. We see their validity when we begin to grow in the virtues, especially in humility and love. For those seeking to develop a life of prayer and grow in union with God, the trick is not to be too attached to mystical experiences or to seek them or cling to them. One must accept them graciously and be at peace, moving on and persevering in prayer even when such experiences are absent. It is the Giver of these gifts we love, not the gifts themselves. We should always be seeking to strengthen our love of God, regardless of what we "get out of" our time in prayer.

Teresa taught that the sacred humanity of Jesus is our way to him. It should never be willfully rejected for any reason, as some people during her life argued was necessary for more profound prayer.

As for women learning mental prayer, she countered that if, as many authorities then claimed, women should stick to their Our Fathers, Hail Marys, and spinning, was there anything wrong with them paying attention to the words they spoke and to whom they were saying these Our Fathers and Hail Marys? Loving attentiveness in vocal prayer, she argued, is already mental prayer.

And how could women (or anyone) be expected to love a Lord they didn't know? How could they know him without spending time with him? "Mental prayer is nothing more than making time to be alone with the One who we know loves us," she said. Furthermore, the Lord is within each of us, and he should not be left alone there like a neglected guest.

She believed in the importance of study to grow in the spiritual life, and she urged those who were serious about following this path to "consult learned men." At the same time, she inspired many of the learned men she consulted to seek God in mental prayer themselves. As she wrote in *The Interior Castle*, "It is more important to love much than to think much."

Teresa was a contemplative nun, and she would always defend the contemplative life against anyone who thought the active life was somehow more important. However, she was also a very active woman engaged in the work and practicalities of founding a new religious order. This meant establishing seventeen religious houses for women and, with her friend and cofounder St. John of the Cross, as many monasteries for men. She knew the fruit of the contemplative life was "good works, my daughters, good works." Therefore, the perfect soul united to God would be a balanced ellipse: the Martha of service at one with her sister, the Mary of prayer.

....

What was foundational for Teresa was this: Jesus is the Friend. As he told his followers, "I no longer call you servants. Instead, I call you friends" (Jn 15:15). Teresa recognized and taught that the life of prayer is friendship with the Lord.

Her own relationship with Jesus was marked by striking tenderness and mutuality. One night Teresa met a beautiful child on the stairs. The little one asked, "What is your name?" Teresa answered, "I am Teresa of Jesus." The little boy replied, "Then I am Jesus of Teresa!"

Teresa once wrote to Jesus:

> Well do I know that you will discover yourself portrayed
> in my heart
> So lifelike drawn
> It will be a delight to behold yourself so well painted.

Another time she exclaimed, "I am for my Beloved and my Beloved is for me."

Her friendship with the Lord was authentic and real. She even let Jesus know how she really felt when she was exasperated while trying to serve him. Once, traveling in pouring rain, she slipped off the back of a cart and fell in the mud. She complained to the Lord, "If this is how you treat your friends, Lord, no wonder you have so few of them!" Yet the mission of her new Order of Discalced Carmelites was to gather a number of "trusty ones" for the Lord who had so few friends.

Later in life she experienced what has come to be known as the Transverberation of St. Teresa. An angel came and pierced her heart with a flaming dart that filled her with pain and love unbearably sweet. She also experienced the "mystical marriage" with Christ — union with God.

Pope St. Paul VI declared Saint Teresa a Doctor of the Church in 1970, calling her "The Doctor of Prayer." More recently, in August 2024, her body was exhumed and found to be still incorrupt.

Given what I have said so far, you might feel intimidated by Saint Teresa. Yet she is said to have been charming, winning over anyone who talked with her. She was wise in the ways of prayer, but she was also funny and witty and real. Her writings reveal someone who was very human.

"Oh, mi padre," she once wrote to her spiritual director, Fr. Jerome Gracián. "A terrible thing happened to me! … a large salamander or lizard got in between my tunic and bare arm, and it was the mercy of God that it didn't get in somewhere else, for I think I would have died, judging how I felt. But my brother got hold of it at once and when he threw it away, it hit Antonio Ruiz right in the mouth."

You can see she was far from being distant, impervious, and aloof, as we might think of such a holy person!

To Brother Juan de la Miseria, who rendered her portrait, she exclaimed, "God forgive you Fray Juan. You've made me ugly and blear-eyed!"

She was a strong believer in daily recreation for her sisters.

She often sang, danced, and played tambourine at such times, delighting everyone. This is also how she and her sisters welcomed new nuns to the convent, with singing and playing tambourines and castanets. After all, joy is a sure sign of the presence of the Holy Spirit.

To me, her playfulness and wit make her more alive and human, more relatable and even more credible than if she had walked around in a mystical haze all the time making sage pronouncements. I wish she were more often represented smiling in art, as her friends say she often did in life.

Saint Teresa had a good sense of humor, and she encouraged it in her nuns. She once wrote, "A sad nun is a bad nun … I am more afraid of one unhappy sister than a crowd of evil spirits. … What would happen if we hid what little sense of humor we had? Let each of us humbly use this to cheer others." She also said, "God save us from sour-faced saints."

She was passionate for God and the Church. The Reformation distressed her deeply. She felt as though Jesus was being crucified all over again by his own followers, with his Church breaking apart. Saint Teresa was concerned that Jesus needed friends since so many were betraying him by tearing the Church apart. She wanted to raise up "trusty friends" for him.

She believed prayer, even the simple inner silence of contemplative prayer (spending time with Jesus and loving him), both made reparation to him for his loss of friends and also had the power to heal the Church and the world by bringing on an outpouring of God's grace. It seemed to her as if the one who prays quietly opens the gates of heaven for the benefit of all.

She believed in the power of contemplative prayer to accomplish great things, because it releases more of God's grace into the world through souls open to him in prayer. This gave urgency to her work to see him befriended in the deepest way possible: contemplative prayer that has the potential to lead one to union with God.

Saint Teresa's order, the Carmelites, was a religious community founded in the mid-twelfth century on Mount Carmel in the Holy Land, where the Prophet Elijah had once lived. In the center of their scattered hermit cells, the first monks built a chapel they named for the Blessed Virgin Mary, where they gathered for daily Mass. Like Elijah, they listened for God in silence and strove to be living, passionate witnesses of his presence.

The Carmelites meditated in their hearts, reflecting Our Lady from deep within and cherishing the Word of God. They called themselves the Brothers of Our Lady of Mt. Carmel. Mary's brothers sought to live out her life of prayer, "pondering the law of the Lord day and night" (from the Rule of St. Albert, the primitive Rule of Carmel). The motto of the Carmelites is the cry of Elijah: "I am burning with jealous love for the Lord, the God of Hosts" (1 Kgs 19:10, more often translated, "With zeal I have been zealous for the Lord God of Hosts").

With Mary, the Carmelites cry out, "My soul proclaims the greatness of the Lord" (Lk 1:46). And they strive to imitate her contemplative heart: "And as for Mary, she treasured all these words and continually pondered over them" (Lk 2:19).

This was Teresa's spiritual family, the order she was called to reform and bring back to its original simplicity. Yet the writings Saint Teresa left us on prayer make clear that the way of inner prayer is not only for priests, friars, and nuns; it is for everyone.

Teresa of Jesus was only a little nun hidden in a convent, but she knew when she looked out her window that the stars and all the universe were hers because Jesus shares his reign with us in prayer, and she was humbly united to him, wanting only his joy. He happily poured out his graces and wisdom on her humble soul.

In all that she did, Saint Teresa left us a beautiful treasure map to lead us to the Pearl of Great Price. Through her writing and teaching, we can discover the Treasure in the Field (see Mt 13:44), which we find tucked in the depths of our own hearts, waiting to be discovered — the kingdom of Heaven, the Lord within.

....

Saint Teresa said she never knew what it was to pray with satisfaction until the Lord himself taught her what she named "The Prayer of Recollection." If you want, Jesus and Saint Teresa can teach you this method of prayer, too.

The Prayer of Recollection as a method is so simple that it almost seems it is not a method at all, but merely a scaffold for silence. Yet given its importance in Saint Teresa's life and the life of her order, it would appear that the Prayer of Recollection is much more than it seems. A Sign of the Cross, an examination of conscience, an act of contrition, an Our Father, and then … what? What do we do after we run out of words to the prayers? With the help of St. Teresa of Jesus, who learned this prayer from the Lord, I hope to answer these questions.

If you have a desire to pray more deeply, to grow exponentially in love, to be connected to God more profoundly, then this prayer is perfect for you. This little book will show you how to pray this way. My hope is that this book will help you to make a good start in practicing the Prayer of Recollection and inspire you to make it a solid habit as the cornerstone of a strong life of prayer.

As we go forward, each section of this book will lay out an aspect of the Prayer of Recollection in focus, giving suggestions on how to put it into practice, as well as some basic discoveries of Saint Teresa about prayer. I have also included simple step-by-step instructions for this method of prayer that you can use and re-use as you learn. Here and there are touches of prayerful imagination to help bring you more deeply into an encounter with Christ in perhaps new ways. And if you are feeling at all intimidated, be assured: If you make a beginning, he will reciprocate. If you are persistent, he will do all the rest for you.

Saint Teresa will be with us as we set out on this journey on the Royal Road of prayer. May we feel, at least figuratively, the brush of her habit and the warm clasp of her hand as she leads us to our hearts where our King is enthroned. And then may she lead us outward to pour out the love we have received from the Lord in prayer. As she said, we have everything to gain. "Whoever has not begun the practice of prayer, I beg for the love of the Lord not to go without so great a good. There is nothing here to fear but only something to desire."

Chapter Two

The Royal Road of Prayer

[Mental prayer] is the Royal Road to Heaven."
— The Way of Perfection

Saint Teresa called mental prayer "the Royal Road." She believed that this way of prayer was established by Jesus our king as a way to lead souls to him. Some people of Teresa's time were really afraid to take the road of mental prayer because they thought it was too dangerous, fraught with demonic deceptions. In their fear, they warned others away from it as well. Still today, many Christians see deep prayer as too esoteric, when it is actually as pure and simple as it can be.

Instead of running away from mental prayer, Teresa advised that we should run away from the people who discourage us from it as fast as we can. She had to emphasize again and again that prayer was the Royal Road — not only the quickest, but the safest way to union with God. "Do not be frightened, daughters," she begged her sisters, "to begin this Divine Journey which is the Royal Road to Heaven. A great Treasure is gained by traveling this road." She wanted it understood that we are meant to travel it and that it is open to all of us.

It's not necessarily the easiest road. It takes discipline and, at times, courage to stay on it through all the stages of spiritual metamorphosis which the soul experiences along the way. It is an epic journey, and there are periods of aridity and darkness, and times when we must face ourselves as we truly are, especially when we find ourselves on the rockier or steeper parts of the road. Yet Saint Teresa urges us to remember at these times that no price is too high for the Treasure we seek.

And although the way may not always be easy, we can be assured that we will never be alone on the way. We join a great company. Along the road, we will see the sandal prints of many Carmelite saints and other holy people who traveled this way before us. They will accompany and help us. Since we are all connected in the Communion of Saints, when we embark on this Royal Road, we will also spiritually travel with the living all over the world who walk this road with us.

Yes, the reward is vast, but that does not mean the way to it is beyond you. It is not beyond you. Only begin and grace will accompany you with every step.

. . . .

The Sacred Humanity of Jesus

"I see clearly that if we expect to please Him and receive an abundance of His graces, God desires that these graces must come to us from the hands of Christ, through His most Sacred Humanity, in which God takes delight."

— Meditations on the Song of Songs

On Easter day, Jesus showed the disciples his wounds and invited them to touch him, to eat and drink with him. He wanted them to know he wasn't a ghost. But I also think he wanted to reiterate something of the utmost importance in the spiritual life of a Christian: that Our Lord is a real person. After the Resurrection, he is just as real as he was before his death, the same man the disciples experienced and traveled with during his ministry, still their same holy Friend. Yet now, after he has risen from the dead, they see him with his glory revealed. His disciples were not having a vision that first Easter Sunday, but actual contact with the physical Jesus.

From the very beginnings of Christianity, there has always been the temptation among people of prayer to try to relate to Jesus solely as spirit. Saint Teresa saw this tendency, and she taught adamantly that the way to true intimacy with the Lord is through his sacred humanity. We are not angel spirits, but human beings. Our humanity, his humanity, is our way to him who became incarnate for us. This never means in any way that we should downplay Jesus' divinity. The Incarnation should be our guide here. He became human without loss of his divinity, as we know. He became one with us and sacrificed himself for us so that we might share in his divinity. He is still for us now a real and accessible person.

If we put this understanding into practice, we will long to be "frequently conversing in secret with him who we know loves us," as Teresa said. The Christian life is a life of friendship with Jesus in his sacred humanity — with him who shares our human lives with us. We too should look at him, touch him, and hear his voice as alive and active — and we can do this in prayer.

Ask him now: "Stay, Lord. Be near. Be real to me."

....

Friendship with Jesus
"He is a true Friend." — Life

Friendship with the Lord is mutual and reciprocal. Sometimes it's hard to think of God that way, as wanting mutuality with us, or of us being capable of such a thing. However, he does. Even though Jesus is Divine, even though Teresa reminds us to treat him with reverence and respect (she often called him "Your Majesty"), she urged treating Jesus as a Friend and allowing him to treat us as his friends.

He encouraged this type of relationship with himself when he told his disciples, "I no longer call you servants but instead, friends" (Jn 15:15). He responds to our friendship in the way he treats us. At times, and I know it sounds preposterous, he even acts as if we are equals with him. He does this in the way he gives himself to us. As his friends, we will experience this directly in prayer. He will sit at our feet; he will come as a child asking for our love, a parent seeking a lost youth, a pleading lover, a devoted brother. And yet he is beyond all that is, a fathomless deep. He is the King of the Universe, yet he takes us by the hand as if we were his cherished childhood friends. It's astonishing, the humility with which he approaches us and the immeasurable graces he shares with us.

But then he did say, "Whoever does the will of God is my brother, my sister, my mother" (Mk 3:35). You are brother, sister, mother, friend of the King of Heaven, and you can join him among the stars.

We know God doesn't need anything, that he is complete and perfect in himself. Yet he does want us. He longs for each of us intensely. He will almost seem as if he needs us. Such is his love that it is sometimes difficult to fully accept. However, once he makes you know it, you won't be able to deny its reality.

In friendship with him we will learn to let ourselves be loved. We will know this on deeper and surer levels all the time until this knowledge is rock solid in us. We will want to give ourselves to him, less and less for our own sake, but more and more because we want to make our Friend happy and because his smile is the sweetest.

Someday you and the Lord will be two best friends who will deny one another nothing. Where does that put the two of you? At a stalemate? No, it puts you together. It makes you one. Saint Teresa called this the union of wills with God. And "what more do we desire from such a good friend at our side?" as Teresa wrote in her Life.

....

Making Friends with Jesus

"The soul is at first like someone who is just beginning to form a friendship, and it must spend time in silence with the One who is its beloved."

— The Interior Castle

This concept of friendship with the Lord is one of Saint Teresa's most engaging insights. All the rules, benefits, and sacrifices of friendship apply. It sounds so simple — and it is. But if we stay with it for a while, we will soon detect a change in our relationship with the Lord. We will have a sense of freshness and renewal, of a new intimacy with him.

How do we actually make friends with Jesus? Saint Teresa suggests that the best way is to ask him, humbly, for his friendship.

Do this now. Ask him.

Next, start spending time with him. Try to address your thoughts to him. Invite him into your day as you go about your tasks. Talk to him. Take him with you when you go places. Serve him when you see him. Maybe he is standing with a sign on the corner needing something to eat. Maybe he is a child needing your full attention. Tell him good night as you close your eyes to sleep. Let him surround you in the quiet.

In every way, regard him in all that you do, for "the Lord

moves among the pots and pans," as Saint Teresa reminds us. We put in a little effort, and he pours his love into our whole lives. You don't have to talk him into it; he wants to.

In friendship with Jesus, we will see more than ever before that our Friend is patient and kind. He really is gentle and humble of heart. His yoke is easy, and his burden is light, just as he said (see Mt 11:28–30). Even when he must correct us, his correction is kind and never destructive. Repentance is sweet with him, and humility is light. His mercy makes us able to understand any hurt we have caused, to bear it, and to do better.

The closer we get to the Lord, the closer we want to be. We will never want to leave his company. He will begin to teach us, often without our knowing how he does so. We will notice small changes, shifts in our thinking, an unexpected growth in compassion, an ease of communion with him over time. We will notice beauty more, and we will easily see the good in people we encounter.

The sense of his presence with and within us will become so important to us that we would give our lives rather than lose it. It will become part of who we are. It will be our joy. Teresa encourages us:

> Imagine that this Lord himself is at your side and see

> how lovingly and how humbly he is teaching you — and, believe me, you should stay with so good a friend for as long as you can before you leave him. If you become accustomed to having him at your side, and if he sees that you love him to be there and are always trying to please him, you will never be able, as we put it, to get rid of him, nor will he ever fail you.

As with so many things, we make a beginning, and he will respond to us. He is already here knocking.

Open the door.

....

God Is Within Us

"We need no wings to go in search of God, but have only to find a place where we can be alone and look upon him present within us.

— The Way of Perfection

Teresa had a vision of the human soul as a beautiful castle with many rooms. She saw that as the soul makes progress in prayer and grows spiritually, she moves through these rooms toward the center. Each room represents a different facet or phase of growth in the spiritual life. When one enters the innermost room of the castle, she finds the Lord enthroned there in her own heart.

"And the door to this castle is prayer."

Then Jesus revealed to his friend Teresa, with a love she could not describe, that he also contains this castle within himself. So in a mysterious way, we are in him and he is in us, just as he is in the Father and the Father is in him (see Jn 14:11).

The Lord has come under our roof. What should we do?

Maybe we are worried the house is not clean. Maybe we think it is not fit for company. Oh, please don't go and spend your whole time with him rushing around trying to clear the table or close doors to hide messes! Don't leave him sitting in the living room by himself. Be with him and ask him what you can get for him. Just move all those dishes aside and sit down with your Friend. He is all that matters. And you are all that matters to him. Anyway, he is really good at cleaning, and he will probably help with that mess you're worried about. He is that kind of friend.

Go to him now, quickly. Run up the steps and into the house to meet him. See how his face lights up when he sees you? That's it. Smile back.

....

Prayer Is a Work of the Church

"Be occupied in prayer for those who would be defenders of the Church and for preachers and for learned men who protect her from attack."

— The Way of Perfection

There is a stained-glass window at Little Flower Basilica in San Antonio, Texas, that shows Carmelite nuns in prayerful procession. Each of them carries something: One holds the world, another holds the Church, one a lantern, and so on. On the opposite side of the basilica, there is a similar window showing the Carmelite Friars. These windows represent in art what the Carmelite charism of prayer does in the world. You are doing this too when you pray.

A soul in prayer becomes an open window for the out-streaming of God's grace into the world for everyone and for the good of the Church. We know from the Gospel that Jesus gives his power of mercy into our hands, as he did when he sent out his disciples to proclaim the Kingdom of God and to heal. He is sending your soul on his errands, opening your heart so he can come through you to the world.

In our humble disposal of ourselves at his feet, heaven rushes into this suffering world. We may not know who hears in their hearts, "Don't be afraid. I am here with you. I love you. I am here." But we can trust that the gentle voice of the Spirit comes to someone somewhere. Travel by heart throughout the world with the Lord, touching every face, blessing every soul.

One of Saint Teresa's outstanding daughters, St. Teresa Benedicta of the Cross, said it this way: "Through the power of the Cross you can be present wherever there is pain, carried there by your compassionate love, by that very love which you draw from the Divine Heart. That love enables you to spread everywhere the Most Precious Blood in order to ease pain, save, and redeem."

How does this work? You don't have to think, "I am spiritually doing this or that." No, only stay hidden in the Lord, resting in his presence in trust. We can actively petition the Lord for priests, for peace, for souls to be saved. However, we can also be in deep silence simply open to the love of God, allowing him to do with us and our open hearts whatever he wants to do, trusting that he will act.

So, pray like Teresa. Open wide the gates of heaven in your soul, until the knowledge of God fills the earth as water fills the sea. Give yourself to him who loves to work wonders through his children. Prayer is always life-giving; its grace will heal you, too.

One of my fellow Carmelites calls prayer "putting more love

into the world." That is what we are doing, and this is a work of the Church. Teresa believed this so strongly that she founded her order to do this necessary work.

....

The Four Waters of Prayer

"Well now, let us speak of this heavenly water that in its abundance soaks and saturates this entire garden." — Life

Saint Teresa used the analogy of watering a garden to explain the phases of growth in prayer in a brief and simple way.

As beginners in mental prayer, we have to haul water from a well to water our soul gardens. It's hard training. But when the Lord sees us being consistent, working hard and staying motivated, he helps us by giving us a windlass — a water wheel that turns and brings up water, pouring it out for us from the dippers attached to it, which eases our workload considerably.

Later he makes a flowing stream water our garden of prayer. He has almost completely taken over the watering himself. Prayer becomes much easier now because of the inflow of his grace.

Last, it just rains. We have nothing at all to do with it anymore but to receive the rain as flowers grow in our soul for the Lord. He has removed all effort. We call this "infused contemplation." Now he picks his flowers, fruit, and herbs with joy. Then what does he do? He pours them into your lap.

As you have given yourself to him, he now gives himself to you.

Chapter Three

Praying the Prayer of Recollection

A person can, at will, enter into recollection, and, with little effort in the beginning, achieve the habit of doing so.

— The Way of Perfection

Choose a quiet place where you can be alone with God. It should be a comfortable, non-distracting place where you can relax. This can be a room in your house, the adoration chapel at your parish, your hotel room when traveling, or wherever you are, as long as you can have quiet and solitude without being disturbed.

Turn off notifications on your phone and set your ringer on "silent." Don't worry about how to sit. Our teacher Saint Teresa didn't mention a particular posture for this prayer.

However, in order to prepare for this prayer, we will need to be physically relaxed. If we are too rigid, we will be more tense and distracted. If we are too slouchy, we may get sleepy. So just sit comfortably with your back supported and relatively straight so you can be at ease and alert at the same time. Try not to fidget. This may be hard at first, but Saint Teresa says our bodies will come under our command in a few days of practice. "We will see that little by little, the soul gains mastery over the body and the senses."

It's OK to gently shift positions if your foot falls asleep or if you become uncomfortable.

Enclose yourself in time. When you prepare for mental prayer, set a timer. How long should you pray? This depends on your circumstances and also on where you are in your prayer journey. If you are new to mental prayer, try starting with five minutes per session. Eventually you could work up to spending ten, fifteen, and then thirty minutes in the prayer of recollection per day, which is the standard recommendation for a serious lay person. It seems like a lot, but it becomes easier, and over time it will be something you want to do. You could, if pressed in your schedule, break this up to two fifteen-minute periods at different times of day (which, as a young mother, I often had to do).

Setting a timer may seem like an artificial imposition on

something that is holy and personal, but it doesn't have to be like that. Try thinking of the timer as a fence to hold your silence and solitude, a wall for your garden of prayer. Saint Teresa would have had a little bell rung by one of the nuns (or maybe it was a castanet) to let the household know when it was time to move to the next part of their day. That way they could give themselves fully to prayer or whatever else they were doing, knowing they weren't missing anything or having to wonder what time it was. The bell would call them at the right time. Then they could be fully present, in tune with God freely during each section of the day.

So, set a timer. I recommend a gentle sound for the alarm — nothing startling. Avoid timers that tick loudly. Now that your time is set, you can go into your garden and shut the gate, ready to pray to your Father in secret. "You are a garden enclosed, my sister, my bride; / a garden enclosed, a fountain sealed" (Song 4:12).

And so we enclose our souls in this little bit of time for Jesus alone. Once you have shut the gate, you are free to let go of what is outside. Let him settle there with you. Hear him say, "Open your heart to me."

....

Settling Down

"Give me the grace to recollect myself in the little heaven of my soul where you have established your dwelling. There you let me find you, there I feel that you are closer to me than anywhere else, and there you prepare my soul quickly to enter into intimacy with you. ... Help me, O Lord, to withdraw my senses from exterior things, make them docile to the commands of my will, so that when I want to converse with you, they will retire at once, like bees shutting themselves up in the hive in order to make honey."

— The Way of Perfection

Most of Saint Teresa's days were calm, quiet, and well-ordered — though at times she had a lot on her mind and much work to do, and sometimes she was traveling. I think she would be concerned for us in the Information Age. We live with constant interruptions, always rushing to keep up as if we were in a race. We are drawn to the lure of technology, distracted by over-connectedness. Many of us struggle with a pervasive sense of overload, concern, and anxiety.

Saint Teresa taught us to calm our minds and senses as we prepare for prayer. I think our present generation has to work on that a little harder than hers did, so I'm including some suggestions.

Saint Teresa recommended going for a walk or doing some spiritual reading, especially from one of the Gospels, before settling in for prayer. These are good ways to quiet our inner selves and become recollected. She said she was able to become recollected more quickly reading the Gospels than with any other reading. I like to read the Gospel from the day's Mass, as I find that to be a perfect, grace-filled start for prayer of any kind.

If you still have trouble with your focus once you are sitting quietly, or if stillness causes you anxiety, or if you have many worries that disturb your peace, here are a few things to try.

First of all, close your eyes. This is an important part of withdrawing from the outside world and drawing your awareness inward.

Next, you might find it helpful to go slowly over the words of a short prayer in your mind, keeping your eyes closed, trying to be receptive to God's presence. Or you can mentally repeat the names of Jesus and Mary to help you settle.

As you begin to quiet your heart and mind, listen to the sounds around you. If you are blessed with a silent house or a quiet chapel, these sounds will be small. Mentally note them, starting with the farthest away. Maybe a dog barks from a neighbor's yard down the street. Someone is mowing in the distance. A car drives by. Now bring your awareness closer. Maybe you hear birds singing, children playing next door, wind in the trees outside your window, a sprinkler or the chanting of cicadas, perhaps. How about sounds in your house or wherever you are right now? A clock ticking, a washing machine swishing, the refrigerator humming, the dog drinking its water in the kitchen.

Listen. What sounds are in your room? The ceiling fan, the air coming on … your own breathing.

Speaking of breathing, you might take a few deep breaths: in through your nose, out through your mouth. Make the last exhale long and slow.

Put all your worries in a little pile to leave here with Jesus, like sandy seashells collected on the beach. Let him wrap them up and put them away while you dust off your hands. Leave them with him while you pray. He will take care of you.

And now that you are truly alone, daughter, son, love of God's life, make the Sign of the Cross.

Ah, here he is now.

Smile.

See him smile back.

....

Go Within Yourself

"Shut yourselves up in this little heaven of your souls where he ever dwells who made both the heaven within them and the earth without, and accustom yourselves to take your eyes off, and to withdraw from, those things by which our external senses are distracted."

— The Way of Perfection

You may be wondering how to go within yourself. First, Saint Teresa wants us to know that our souls are more precious than we think they are. As I mentioned earlier, God showed her the human soul as a clear, crystalline castle, shining with gold, brighter than any diamond, brilliantly bejeweled and indescribably beautiful. She says maybe it sounds silly for her to tell us to go within ourselves because we are already ourselves. Maybe it seems like she is telling us to go into a room we are already in.

However, she notes that some people never do go within themselves. She thought it was sad that so many of us wander around the outside but never go in, leaving the Lord walking the halls of our castle alone. She asks us to enter the castle. Imagine its beauty, fit for a king, and go in.

When I first learned about Teresa's vision of the soul as a beautiful castle, I loved the idea, and I believed it completely. As she said, this is good for us to think about to understand how precious and beautiful our souls are to the Beloved. Yet I personally would be uncomfortable in a castle, even if I am one. I'm more of a front porch or a kitchen table kind of person, or a room-full-of-books person, or a walk-along-the-beach person. Surely there is room for a beach? Or maybe a beautiful meadow, or a garden.

When I first began practicing this prayer, I needed things to be less formal. I needed my castle to be a comfortable sort of place, and for the King to dress down for me a little and look more comfortable too. Here's what I found out: he will! He wants you to be with him, close to him and familiar. He wants to meet you where you are and where you can be yourself. After all, he was poor when he was here on earth walking among us. Yes, he is truly more glorious than any earthly king could ever be, so much more beautiful than any of us are capable of imagining in his bright finery. But when he was on earth, he dressed in plain home-woven clothes and simple sandals. He would be comparable to a guy in old jeans, a t-shirt, and sneakers today. That comfortable image of him made me a lot more easy with him at first, when I was not too sure about him yet.

So imagine this wonderful place — this garden, this clear castle, this house, this inside of your heart — any way that makes sense to you. Let it be a place where you would like to be with the Lord. He does not mind how you decorate. He just wants to be with you. I think Saint Teresa wouldn't mind this approach much, either. She wants the same thing for you, to go within your beautiful Christian soul and to experience the "intimate sharing between friends" Jesus offers you there.

Imagine yourself coming up the path, unlocking the gate, opening the door.

He will be there.

....

Examination of Conscience

"As to my evil deeds and my sins, he hid them at once." — Life

When we come before the Friend who we know loves us, it is important that we make an examination of conscience. This is so we can remove anything that stands between us and him, trusting he will then remove it from us.

If we have failed a friend, we aren't going to show up to our coffee date with her (or him) and pretend nothing has happened. We don't ignore problems; we address them because we care about our friendship. We love our friend, and we want to be a good friend, so we say, "I'm sorry I forgot to call you," or we say, "I think I hurt your feelings when we were all talking. I'm sorry, I should have realized."

The Friend knows we are little and prone to weakness. He knows. He loves our trust and the love we have for him, that we open our hearts and admit our wrongs before him. So unburden your heart and don't be ashamed. As you look over your day, tell him everything without fear: the moments when you lost your temper, failed to help someone you know you should have, were lax in your duties at work or home; the ways in which you were selfish, prideful, dishonest, or mean. Tell him everything without fear. You show great trust in his mercy and love this way.

It has been more productive and transformative for me to regard myself with a kind of detached affection when I see my sins and failings as I would those of a small child. I have a tendency to be intensely ashamed of any wrong I commit, which I think is a kind of self-absorption and pride. Shame is unhelpful in trying to change or let myself be changed. I can waste a lot of time being shocked at myself when Jesus isn't. He knows me better than I know myself, and nothing I do surprises him. As Saint Thérèse, the Little Flower, said, when we are little, we don't have far to fall, and we know we will soon be scooped up in our Father's arms and comforted.

Unburden your faults to Jesus who is here with you. Then pray an Act of Contrition, either the traditional one or one that is in your own words.

And now he is gently washing your face. He does this with so much quiet mercy and love. He does this so you can shine again. He loves to see that.

Feel your face cool and clean.

Now take his hands. He is offering them to you. How do his hands feel in yours?

Look at him.

Let him look at you.

"You are wholly beautiful, my love, / perfect and unblemished" (Song 4:7).

....

Pray the Lord's Prayer

"As we repeat the Our Father so many times ... let us delight in it."

— The Way of Perfection

Now that your heart is quiet and clear, pray the Lord's Prayer (the Our Father). Pray it along with Jesus, who is here with you. Pray it slowly and reflectively with him, line by line. Let him teach it to you anew.

Allow yourself to ponder it, not doing a lot of thinking, but praying attentively, conscious that Jesus is praying it with you, loving you, hoping and asking his Father with you. Feel his carpenter's hands in yours, calloused, warm, and strong.

Do any words or phrases of the prayer stand out to you? Do any images cross your mind as you pray and savor the lines of this prayer of Jesus? Maybe you want to mentally repeat any resonant words or phrases, or briefly explore any related imagery that has come to you as you pray. Consider in a receptive way what the Holy Spirit has brought to your attention, what God is saying to you with that word, phrase, or image.

What does Jesus do as he prays with you? Maybe he tucks your hair behind your ear so he can see you better. He wants to look at you.

Do you sense any resistance in yourself to any particular line or word of the prayer? Ask Jesus why.

The most important thing is to pay attention and stay connected to the Lord as you silently pray from the heart.

You will find that once you slow down and pray it reflectively, the Lord's Prayer is so rich you could spend your whole prayer time with it alone, focused and attentive to God. Since God's word is living and effective, never returning to him void, unfailingly doing what he sends it to do, this will always be a fruitful prayer when you take it to heart.

Saint Teresa once spoke with an elderly nun who was said to be a very holy, prayerful woman. Teresa determined, speaking with her, that this nun had "reached perfection," or union with God, even though she was completely bound to the Our Father, which made up the entirety of her prayer. Teresa believed that praying the Lord's Prayer enlarges the soul and makes it fit to serve God better.

Let the Lord's prayer be real and authentic for you, truly making each petition before our beautiful Father, who listens and responds. Take time to savor the words in the presence of God.

A novice once asked Saint Teresa how to become a contemplative.

Teresa answered: Pray the Our Father, but take an hour to say it.

Even if it doesn't take you an hour, try praying the Lord's Prayer with uncomplicated, simple regard. Just mentally repeat the words slowly, keeping the eyes of your soul on the Lord. As Saint Teresa said, "It is more important to love much than to think much."

The Lord loves to hear you say this prayer. See that look on his face? Enchanted. "Show me your face, / let me hear your voice; / for your voice is sweet, / and your face is so lovely" (Song 2:14).

....

Look at Jesus

"But above all things, I want to impress upon you that, when we are speaking to him, we should look at him and remain in his presence, and not turn our backs upon him."

— The Way of Perfection

When we are speaking with a friend, we look at her or him. We don't want our friend to think we aren't listening. As Teresa points out, Jesus is looking at us when we speak to him. We should do the same for him. She expresses this very firmly: "All difficulties in prayer can be traced to one cause: praying as if God were absent."

We never want to do that, and it's all too easy to fall into. Yet how do we look at someone we can't see? Saint Teresa suggests that we find an image of Jesus that we like, one we can talk to and pray with. We should keep it near us. Over time, this image of the Lord will migrate into our heart, be assimilated, and carried within us, always accessible. You can also use an imaginative image of the Lord in the same way. "Do that which best stirs you to love," Teresa counsels.

What can stir us to love more than looking at Jesus? Try looking at him now. What does he look like, smell like, sound like? What does it feel like to hug him? Spend some time imagining him in a way that lets him be most real to you.

To me, imagination facilitates an encounter with God just as the words of a prayer do: by focusing the will, the mind, and the heart on him. Early in my conversion, imagining Jesus made him more real and relatable to me.

Don't be afraid to be receptive to your prayerful imagination. The imaginative part is the work of your mind, but the encounter itself is real. Saint Teresa said she couldn't form a good picture of Jesus' face in her mind. Neither can I, really. This is a good thing though. Try imagining him only lightly, just the one or two details you need to set you in his presence — maybe his feet in their sandals, any scars or calluses on his fingers, the way his hair falls, or, as Saint Teresa mentioned, "his dark and lovely eyes."

The best part of letting yourself imagine him is really what is behind it: your loving regard of him. And that can be done without imagining much or even without imagining at all. This little touch of imagery is like a bridge you can use to cross into a livelier awareness of his real presence with you.

So envision Jesus in the way that speaks best to you, or use an image of him that you have. Allow him to come to you now.

Look how happy he is to see you. What does he say, if anything? What happens for you when you see him? Does he say anything to you? If he does not seem to speak to you, Saint Teresa advises, "Our Lord wishes us at such a time to offer him our petitions and to place ourselves in his presence; he knows what is best for us."

It takes practice to learn to be receptive to his guidance and to know when he wants us to be silent, and when he is waiting for us to speak or tell him our petitions. Don't worry if you don't understand this right now. I am confident that you will with time, practice, and, of course, his help.

Remember to imagine only a little and to keep your silent words simple. We don't want this to become a mental exercise but to be a prayer that is a communion with God. Thus Saint Teresa instructs us, "I am not asking you now to think of him, or to form numerous conceptions of him, or to make long and subtle meditations with your understanding. I am asking you only to look at him. For who can prevent you from turning the eyes of your soul (just for a moment, if you can do no more) upon this Lord?"

....

Talking to Jesus

"Speak to him as a father, ask him favors as from a father; let us tell him our troubles, and beg him to relieve us. Treat him as your father, your brother, and your spouse — sometimes in one way, and sometimes another."

— The Way of Perfection

We should not be irreverent, of course, but we should ask for what we need with confidence. He wants us to do this. We can ask him for anything, trusting his providence.

Especially, ask him to give you himself. "Provided we bear in mind that we are with him, and remember that we are asking for him, and how glad he is to give us what we ask, and how delighted he is to be in our company, he is quite satisfied and does not wish us to split our heads by trying to make long discourses."

....

Interior Silence with Jesus

"He is only waiting for us to look at him!"

— The Way of Perfection

There are several ways to stay present with Jesus even when you're not "talking." As Saint Teresa's friend and cofounder St.

John of the Cross said, "What we need most in order to make progress is to be silent before this great God with our appetite and with our tongue, for the language he best hears is silent love."

In the beginning this is hard to do.

One of the best ways to refocus is to say the Holy Name of Jesus. If you feel yourself mentally wandering, inwardly say his name to bring yourself back to an awareness of his presence within you. Do this as many times as you need to. The Holy Name itself is a prayer.

You may also mentally go over a short set prayer to bring you back to him, such as "Christ, have mercy," or "Sacred Heart of Jesus." Choose something brief that best "stirs you to love."

Be careful not to fire words off one after another. Saint Teresa said, "If they call that prayer — well — words fail me." We want to dive deeper, not merely skip across the surface like a pebble being thrown. If you find yourself going too quickly, slow down; leave a little space between the words. This will help your mind and body to relax and allow you to cultivate an open, receptive disposition.

The most important thing is keeping your attention with Jesus in a way that works for you; his name, his image within you, a little prayer, your simple regard in the quiet, holding his hand or resting in his embrace, breathing in his scent.

Ending Your Prayer Session

"May it please the Lord, sisters, that we may reach the place where we utter this word 'Amen' with full realization of what it signifies and with perfect willingness to give to God what we have promised him."

— The Way of Perfection

Teresa did not say in what way we should close the Prayer of Recollection. I like to end with an everyday Catholic prayer, such as a silent Glory Be or the Hail Mary, and then the Sign of the Cross.

Let him hug and kiss you now, sending you back to your day.

Chapter Four
Tips and Helpful Thoughts

If we accustom ourselves to being inwardly attentive for some days, and try to practice this recollection, the benefits will become clear.

— The Way of Perfection

If you have tried the Prayer of Recollection, you may have noticed that it's simple but not easy to do. This chapter offers tips to improve the experience, as well as encouragement and reassurance of the value of pressing on and growing in this prayer — and in love.

....

Handling Distractions

"The intellect is so wild that it doesn't seem to be anything else than a frantic madman no one can tie down." — The Interior Castle

Distractions tend to distress us, especially at the beginning of learning mental prayer or when we are anxious, upset, or particularly busy in our lives.

As soon as you sit down, your mind goes everywhere. Lists, emotions, conversations past and imaginary, feelings, memories, and wishes come running, waving their arms for attention. Of course, wonderful ideas assail you as well. It's easy to become discouraged or think you aren't suited to mental prayer.

You never know, though, what God is working in your soul as you struggle. Saint Teresa wrote:

> We cannot stop the revolution of the heavens as they rush with velocity upon their course, neither can we control our imagination. When this wanders we at once imagine that all the powers of the soul follow it; we think everything is lost, and that the time spent in God's presence is wasted. Meanwhile, the soul is perhaps entirely united to him in the innermost mansions, while the imagination is in the precincts of the castle, struggling with a thousand

> wild and venomous creatures and gaining merit by its warfare. Therefore we need not let ourselves be disturbed, nor give up prayer, as the devil is striving to persuade us.

I want to emphasize that distractions are normal, and to some extent, in the work of prayer, we will always have them. It's important not to be mad at yourself about distractions. They are what the human mind does. In this prayer, we are training the mind to remain with God in a conscious, sustained way for a time, with the "Friend who we know loves us."

Our Friend knows our minds are unruly, that we are anxious and worried about so many things. He knows. You have chosen the better part, though, and it will not be taken from you. He will complete the good work he has begun in you, as long as he has your commitment and cooperation.

One helpful way I learned to handle distractions was to categorize them as they came up. Name them and dismiss them. Acknowledge the interrupting thought. Mentally say, "Planning," then gently dismiss it and return to your prayer. For an intruding memory, say, "Remembering," and do the same. You could label a thought "Worrying" if you keep thinking of your bills. Draw yourself back without judgment.

All of this takes time and effort. The mind does not want to be trained, and it will throw every possible obstacle in your path — even good, holy thoughts or brilliant ideas. Let them all go. God willing, they will come back to you. Return to focus on God alone.

If we are patient and gentle with our minds as we would be with a puppy who runs away while we are trying to teach it something, we are less likely to waste energy being annoyed. Be kind to your mind, especially if concentrated prayer is new to it. It will come under your control if you persist kindly but firmly. One day you will notice that as soon as you close your eyes, there will be instant inner quiet almost every time.

Settling into prayer will be like walking into a cool, still, and silent chapel on a hot, bustling summer day — your quiet inner chapel where Jesus waits.

You will have God's help. He'll gently turn your face back to himself if you falter, and you'll find you won't want to look away, he is so dear.

....

Making Prayer Time a Habit

"One needs no bodily strength for mental prayer, but only love and the formation of a habit." — Life

Something that helped me a lot in the beginning to be consistent in the habit of prayer was to attach mental prayer to something else I already did every day. Think of routines you already have and see if you can link the Prayer of Recollection to any of these, such as your morning coffee.

Another help is starting small just to get yourself in the habit of always sitting down for some quiet time at a certain time each day. You can start with five minutes, as mentioned earlier. Stay with that short amount of time until you are used to doing this.

Something else I did, and have to do again from time to time, was to clear my schedule of unnecessary activities. It may surprise you how many things you think you have to do that you don't really need to do. The spiritual life requires time. An uncluttered mind and a quiet heart are indispensable, so we want to make that as possible as we can. Jesus doesn't seem to want to just watch us run around or for our minds to be too full of TV or the internet for him to get through our door. He does want our full attention for a while in peace.

Saint Teresa's hope in founding the Discalced Carmelites was in large part to give herself and her spiritual children a well-ordered, quiet place where they could live as simple a life as possible, free of intrusions and distractions, so they could work and pray in peace. Most of us are out in the world, raising children, working, trying to keep up with our responsibilities, staying involved in our communities — all good things to do. Yet we can still take a look at our hectic lives and minds and find ways to make them perhaps a little less hectic, to make room for prayer.

....

Don't Freak Out

"The habit of recollection is not to be gained by force of arms but with calmness."

— The Interior Castle

Don't worry if you miss your prayer time or if you fall away from prayer for a while. The important thing is to take it up again as soon as you can. We all have to start over sometimes.

If you must miss prayer because someone needs you or a duty arises, Saint Teresa said to dedicate that activity to God and move on. If you are sick and miserable, as Saint Teresa was for so many years of her life, just do what you can and lean on others who are able to pray and serve as you cannot. And, of course, offer him your suffering.

If you get out of the habit of prayer, being upset with yourself will not help you grow. But returning to prayer will. Just come back to Jesus. He is still there. He will never leave you or give up on you. Trust him to help you up when you fall, even if you have to go back to hauling water buckets from the well again for a while. He is there to help, sleeves rolled up, hair in a ponytail, holding the bucket and eager for you to get started again. "If you fall sometimes, do not be discouraged, since God is your Father and he will not let you fall. He will stretch out his hand and raise you up as he did with Saint Peter."

....

Falling Asleep

"I often had more trouble keeping awake in prayer than in submitting to the penances imposed upon me. I would go to prayer with the determination to keep awake. ... But I never succeeded. I would be overcome with sleep, and sometimes during the entire hour." — Life

Saint Teresa did not have any specific instruction regarding the problem of falling asleep during prayer, though she did address the issue with compassion. One of her spiritual daughters, St. Thérèse of the Child Jesus and of the Holy Face, spoke of this as well. She wrote: "I don't feel at all distressed. I know that children are just as dear to their parents whether they are asleep or awake and I know that doctors put their patients to sleep before they operate."

If you are falling asleep too often in prayer, here are a few things to consider trying:

- Pray at a different time of day.
- Make sure you are getting enough sleep.
- Try not to eat right before you pray.
- Make sure the room you're in is cool enough, with good ventilation.

Last, if you feel that you are close to dropping off during prayer, pull away from the back of your chair and sit up straight for a while. It's hard when you are drifting comfortably, but it will help you be more alert.

....

Moods

"For see, he endures all things for our sakes, bears our burdens, and stands with us patiently, whatever our moods, faults, or sorrows."

— The Way of Perfection

When you pray, you don't have to feel any particular way. You don't have to not feel any particular way, either.

Instead of advising us to ignore our emotions, Saint Teresa thought we should look at Jesus at a time in his life when he was feeling what we are feeling. She said such is his compassion that even on the way to the garden of Gethsemane, he will turn his agonized face to you and "look upon you with his lovely and compassionate eyes, full of tears, and in comforting your grief will forget his own."

If you are happy, be with him at the scene of his Resurrection. Share in his exultation and let him share in yours. Hear that wonderful laugh of his. Be happy with that joy no one can take from either him or you.

However you are feeling, find him, for he is there. In the Gospels we see our Lord expressing a full range of emotions we can identify with. Let him be real to you and present as he wants to be, right in it with you.

Teresa went so far as to say that, as a wife of her time was expected to reflect the moods of her husband, Jesus seems to do this for us out of love. He wants to weep with those who weep and rejoice with those who rejoice. His love for us causes him to respond to our feelings and to mold himself to us at times. His Majesty seems to lay himself in us as we lay ourselves in him.

The closer we get to the Lord, the more we can reciprocate with him. It is a beautiful thing he lets us do when he lays his troubled head in our lap so we can comfort him, or when he communicates his joy to us, wanting us to feel it too.

....

How to Deal with Aridity

"[In aridity] the great thing for us to do is to embrace the cross. The Lord was deprived of all consolations; they left him alone in his trials. Let us not leave him." — Life

A difficulty you may face in your prayer life, especially once you are well on your way, is aptly called aridity, or dryness. Prayer starts to feel like reading the most boring technical paper you could ever find on a subject you know nothing about and are not interested in, or like doing homework for a class you're terrible at.

Saint Teresa understands from her own experience. She relates that for a time when it came to prayer, "I was more anxious for the hour of prayer to be over than I was to remain there. I don't know what heavy penance I would have gladly undertaken rather than to practice prayer."

Perhaps you have reached this point in prayer. Your joy in prayer is gone. It feels like nothing is happening, or even that prayer is painful and empty. It feels as if God has left you.

Reflect that God is not limited by our personal perception of how "well" we are praying or how we feel about prayer. No matter how we feel, God is still within us in the same place as always, loving us still. We can have faith in that.

If you are struggling with prayer in this way, then this is one of the times you will need that "determined determination" of which Saint Teresa speaks. God is working with purpose in this period of aridity. Be faithful, be strong, take heart, and keep praying.

Saint Teresa herself struggled with terrible aridity for long periods of time. She can relate to your sense of dryness in prayer with great compassion and understanding. She will be leading you through the desert of aridity, helping you find water in surprising places, showing you the desert's secret beauties.

....

Consolations

"God bestows these graces for no other reason than his own choice, into which we have no right to enquire."

— The Interior Castle

The opposites of dry spells in prayer are called consolations. Some people experience them, and some people don't. It's important to be OK either way.

If you do receive consolations, you may sometimes feel a

deep sense of peace and joy, intense love, or even feelings of euphoria when you pray. You may experience the sensible closeness or touch of God on your soul. You may receive flashes of understanding or the unraveling of a difficulty. God may give us this sweetness from time to time.

There is nothing wrong with these things. If consolations do come to you, appreciate them while they last, but don't cling to them or try to perpetuate them yourself. Understand that these experiences come and go. Try to be peaceful and accepting when they stop. These are wonderful gifts that draw us closer to God within, away from the outward show of the world. They help us grow in virtue. Consolations can be healing and inspiring, opening the heart. Yet when these good things are withdrawn, let them go as easily as a breath, with your focus on the Giver, and continue the prayer. In this way, you will be learning to love God more and more for himself, whatever he gives or does not give.

If we practice this easiness about the presence or absence of consolations, we grow immeasurably. God doesn't need to give consolations in order to work in and with our soul. It's up to his discretion and his perfect knowledge of us. He knows exactly what we need.

....

Be Humble and Receptive

"This water does not flow through aqueducts ... and if the spring does not afford it, in vain shall we toil to obtain it. I mean, that though we may meditate and try our hardest, and though we shed tears to gain it, we cannot make this water flow. God alone gives it to whom he chooses, and often when the soul is least thinking of it. We are his, Sisters, let him do what he will with us, and lead us where he will."

— The Interior Castle

Saint Teresa went through a time in her life of prayer that she later looked back on with regret. She had been reading books on contemplative prayer and often saw advice to forget anything earthly, even Jesus' physical body and earthly life, during mental prayer. So for years she had tried to do this. Her growth stalled, but she didn't know why. Finally, God revealed to her what she was doing wrong. While there are states of prayer, especially ecstatic prayer, that remove the mind's ability to do anything at all, even picture anything holy, this experience is not something the soul can or should try to create for itself. It is an all-encompassing experience of God. No self-direction or imagination is possible in these states.

Teresa had had experiences like that. She compared the Lord at these times to a giant and herself to a piece of straw. He will lift up the soul if and whenever he likes. The best way to experience this kind of prayer, she learned from Jesus, was to be humble and receptive to him. He wants us to be humble souls who take the lowest place. The rest is up to him.

So she understood that it was a lack of humility on her part to actively seek to arrive at that state of prayer by her own efforts. Once she knew this and abandoned her previous practice, she quickly became unstuck. She wrote, "What I have come to understand is that this whole groundwork of prayer is based on humility and that the more a soul lowers itself in prayer the more God raises it up."

This receptive, humble attitude reminds me of Psalm 131. The weaned child sits peacefully in his mother's lap, not clamoring for the breast anymore, but sitting in silence and peace, seeking nothing, simply letting his mother hold him and being deeply content in her presence and proximity.

So yes, we should put other things out of our mind when we practice mental prayer, but never the Incarnate Lord — never the Beloved. We can simply be little before God, and content, letting ourselves be loved.

....

Don't Give Up, No Matter What

"[Beginners] should begin well by making an earnest and most determined resolve not to halt until they reach their goal, whatever may come, whatever may happen to them, however hard they may have to labor, whoever may complain of them, whether they reach their goal or die on the road or have no heart to confront the trials which they meet, whether the very world dissolves before them."

— The Way of Perfection

Saint Teresa said those who set out on the Royal Road of prayer must have "determined determination." She was very serious about this.

She had learned this through hard experience, having given up prayer for a long while herself. She did so because of what she later recognized as false humility. It was a period of her life she looked back on as wasted time. Thanks be to God, she resumed prayer even though she was discouraged and thought she was not good enough to continue the path she had begun.

She goes so far as to say: "I know for certain that, if you will only persevere, in the course of a year, or perhaps in six months, by God's help, you will obtain what you desire. See what a short time is required for obtaining so immense a good!"

That's quite a promise.

"Whom are you seeking?" and "What are you looking for?" the Lord asks us.

How would you answer him? Stop a moment and tell Jesus now.

....

Prayer Is a Wellspring in the Heart

"The surest sign that we are keeping these two commandments [love of God and love of neighbor] is that we should really be loving our neighbor; for we cannot be sure if we are loving God, although we may have good reason for believing that we are. But we can know quite well if we are loving our neighbor."

— The Interior Castle

Asked by her nuns to teach them her way of prayer, Teresa wrote for them *The Way of Perfection*. I wonder if her spiritual daughters were surprised that it did not contain much in the way of method in prayer. Only one chapter was given to how to pray the Prayer of Recollection. The rest was almost completely filled with instructions for crafting a life of prayer.

The story of Jesus and the Samaritan woman at Jacob's well (see Jn 4:4–44) illustrates this understanding beautifully. Jesus first asks the woman for a drink. He wants our love so much that it surprises us too, doesn't it? Who and what are we that he would desire anything from us at all?

In the course of the conversation, Jesus reveals himself to the woman as the Messiah: "I who speak to you am he." This is what happens in prayer: He tells us who he is. As Saint Teresa wrote, he begins to reveal to the soul his secrets, his heart, the truth of his being.

Jesus told the woman at the well that he would give her living water. She replied gladly that she wanted that water so she wouldn't have to keep coming to the well. I can't help thinking here of Saint Teresa's analogy of the four waters of prayer, which begins with us having to haul water from the well to water the garden of our souls. Jesus responded to the woman by telling her that the human heart itself wells up as a spring of living water that overflows.

We can't possibly expect to just pray in our prayer corner every day and have nothing outside that time and place begin to change. It has to. We can't give ourselves to prayer without the love we receive streaming out into our daily lives. This living water soaks into our chores, our community life, our work, our speech, our relationships, the service we give freely as we have received the mercy and love of God.

At the well, Jesus told the Samaritan woman about herself,

and she was amazed. It seems he showed her something wonderful besides simply how many husbands and boyfriends she'd had. I have to think he showed her something wonderful about herself and who she was in his eyes. When she rushed into the village to tell others about him, she said, "He told me everything I ever did," rather than, "he told me how many men I have had in my life!" Maybe it is like Nathanael's effusive response elsewhere in the Gospel, when Jesus tells him, "I saw you under the fig tree" (Jn 1:47–49). Jesus saw the Samaritan woman too, and perhaps because of that, she also saw herself as he did.

Then she impulsively ran to share the Treasure she had found: the Lord himself, who tells us who he is and who we are, and who gives us living water.

After her encounter with Jesus at the well, the Samaritan woman learned to worship him in spirit and truth as he said God wanted. She experienced transforming love, going on to live a life of prayer and service, splashing everyone she met with her joy. How could she not? And how could Jesus resist such an open and honest heart?

This is what a life of prayer can produce in us, too. Saint Teresa writes: "It seems to me that one of the greatest consolations a person can have on earth must be to see other souls helped through his own efforts. Then, it seems to me, one eats the delicious fruit of these flowers. Happy are those to whom the Lord grants these favors."

....

Soul Friends

"A good means of knowing God is to speak to his friends."

— The Way of Perfection

It's vital to find other travelers we can talk to along the Royal Road. Seek them out, because when two or three are gathered in his name, he tends to reveal his presence in new and more vivid ways.

Saint Teresa's religious communities were founded on friendship. She wanted her daughters to be friends of God who were in friendship with one another. There must be no social hierarchy or favoritism, she taught. This way we don't miss out on each other, and we build a strong community. "All must be friends, all must be loved, all must be held dear, all must be helped."

She wrote extensively about the upkeep of spiritual friendships and the strong community life so necessary for the spiritual path, especially in Chapter 7 of *The Way of Perfection.* We grow in spirit exponentially within relationships, within community. We refine one another, smoothing one another's rough edges. We learn to forgive, to be patient, to be kind, humble, and open-hearted in our friendships.

In spiritual conversation we support, inspire, motivate, and gently humble one another. We uphold and pray for one another's spiritual progress. We strive to fulfill the commandment of Jesus, that we love one another as he has loved us.

....

Prayer Is a Cup That Overflows

"I hold that love, where present, cannot possibly be content with remaining always the same."

— The Interior Castle

Saint Teresa taught that the spiritual person is "a servant of love," as Fr. Mark O'Keefe, OSB, puts it in his book about Teresa's relational approach to prayer and transformation, *The Intimate Sharing of Friends*. Teresa means authentic, compassionate love, not merely a general, obligatory "love." She would say if you see someone hungry, feed him. If someone needs help, help her. You will begin to serve more and more authentically from the heart, both because you know that is what God wants and because your heart has been enlarged by the Lord. Now you can't help but be compassionate to those who suffer. You give of yourself spontaneously, as a matter of course. Saint Teresa advised us to look for every little opportunity to serve, to help, to do good.

Our experiences of God are "not for our enjoyment but for service." As you grow in prayer, your acts of loving service strengthen your prayer, and your prayer will strengthen your compassion. You will instinctively know what God is calling you to do in service to others. The goal of prayer is to more and more reflect Jesus, giving of ourselves to each person as part of who we are. You will find, as our teacher Saint Teresa did, that "love turns work into rest."

Prayer is a cup that runs over both for ourselves and for other people. It's grace overflowing, extending to a love and compassion for all of life, giving joy to the heart of the Lord. Thus Teresa advises, "Accustom yourself continually to make many acts of love, for they enkindle and melt the soul."

It's important to make contact with God throughout the day, to give him little moments with us, to do small things for him or dedicate to him the tasks we already do, and to speak a word of love to him now and then. Sometimes you may feel pulled into prayer as you are doing other things. Give in to that pull. Let it take you. You can learn to be recollected as you work, doing the normal things you do. Prayer is a cup that runs over, filling our lives until they become a prayer.

Teresa wrote in a stream-of-consciousness style peppered

with charming digressions or sudden exclamations. Many of these were exclamations of praise. Prayer is a cup that overflows, and she brimmed with gratitude, love, and the praises of God. One day you might find yourself in the same condition, calling on the ocean or the sky to praise him in your name because your body and spirit don't seem big enough to contain the praise that fills you past overflowing.

....

Connecting Through the Passion

"I have seen clearly that it is by this door [meditating on Christ's passion] that we must enter, if we wish his sovereign majesty to show us great secrets in the interior castle."

— The Interior Castle

Saint Teresa faced a lot of misunderstanding and alarm from confessors with whom she tried to share her spiritual life. Some told her that her experiences in prayer were from the devil. She cried so much during that time and even said she wanted to die. She was afraid to be alone, and they told her she should not be. She did everything they said, even trying to resist the Lord's graces, but he gave them all the more.

Eventually, she found St. Peter of Alcántara, who did not let her off the hook, which wouldn't have given her peace, but also did not condemn her. She had finally found a spiritual guide both learned and experienced in prayer to help her understand what was happening and to guide her. He gently helped her to see that though her experiences were from the Lord, she had also been selfish and careless in her spiritual life. These mystical experiences were given to her in spite of her faults. She needed grounding. He suggested penance and self-denial, along with meditating on the sorrowful mysteries of the Rosary daily for a month, in order to better come to the Lord through his sacred humanity. She says firmly, "Prayer and self-indulgence don't go together."

She immediately grew from this, and the Lord filled her soul with his graces more than ever before. Therefore, her suggestion to the beginner especially is to meditate on the Lord's Passion, connecting with his humanity there, loving him there. Remember his tears. Feel them smear your own cheek as you embrace him. In your meditations let Jesus be as real and human as possible to you.

Saint Teresa did, however, understand that some people are very sensitive and more upset by the brutal suffering Jesus endured than others are. More sensitive people should only meditate on the Sorrowful Mysteries a couple times a week and not for as long each time as she would recommend to most.

Whenever we meditate on the Passion, Teresa counsels,

"Represent Christ as within yourself and meditate on his sufferings there."

....

Detachment

"He would have you keep back nothing; whether it be little or much, he will have it all for himself, and according to what you know yourself to have given, the favors he will grant you will be small or great."

— The Interior Castle

How do you feel about the word detachment? Do you feel a little resistance in yourself when you hear that a serious spiritual life requires it?

Saint Teresa even talks about detachment from family and friends and detachment from self. She spoke of letting go of friendships that hold us back. This might sound a little scary to us; it is a truth from which we may instinctively shrink. Yet if we wish to grow in prayer, walking the Royal Road, we must come to understand detachment and lose the fear of it. How do we do this?

In detachment we love those around us from a foundation of God's love — from the love he has for them, which is so much more than ours and completely unselfish. Detachment brings us to see through God's eyes, to love with God's heart. It isn't a cold, distant ideal, but letting the Lord be the source of all our love and desires so we come to love each person his way, the way God wants us to love. Teresa says that when we let go of anything or anyone for love of God, once we have discerned it is what he wants, we will receive it back all the more in a purer way if it is God's will. If it is not his will, he will give us peace, and it will be for the other person's good as well as ours. This is truly loving the other person rather than our own pleasure in them.

Saint Teresa must have been a lovely friend to have. She was warm and bright, witty and funny, intelligent and a great conversationalist. Like most of us, sometimes her strengths were her weaknesses, and from the time of her youth until she fully gave herself to prayer, she had to deal with her tendency to become overly attached to people who liked her, to the point of distraction, "thinking of them all the time." This may explain why detachment was so important to her and why she learned about its worth, writing about it often.

We must always work on detachment with love, turning our relationships over to God. One of the best prayers I have ever heard, and one that I pray frequently, is, "Lord, work your will through (name), work your will through me, and let this relationship be what you want it to be." Teresa taught that, in a true friendship guided and shaped by the Holy Spirit, both people grow spiritually and want to see each other pursue the path of prayer and love of God.

As for detachment from self, how can we allow God to transform us if we are unwilling to detach from ourselves? We are so prone to have an idea of ourselves that is not really who we are at all. Our self-knowledge is purified in God. Our worth, our identity is in him. He is the only one who truly knows who we are. Maybe this is what Jesus meant when he said by losing our lives, we find them (see Mt 16:25).

In the context of the life of prayer, this makes deep sense. Sell all you have. Buy the field. Possess the Treasure.

Conclusion

In Brief

When you pray, go into your room, shut the door,
and pray to your Father in Secret.

— Matthew 6:6

The basic steps of the Prayer of Recollection (for repeated use until you learn the prayer) are as follows:

Sit in silence and solitude, setting a timer for your prayer session.

Make the Sign of the Cross.

Take a deep breath, close your eyes, and recollect yourself.

Imagine going within your soul represented as a beautiful castle (or a chapel, a house, a garden, or however you

want to represent your inner self where Jesus lives).
Look at Jesus represented within yourself.
Make an examination of conscience with him.
Pray an Act of Contrition to him.
Pray a slow, reflective Our Father with him.
Hold an interior conversation with the Lord, being receptive to any responses he may have.
With a quiet heart, continue to look at Jesus, striving to remain in a state of loving attentiveness and receptivity to him.
If distracted, gently redirect your attention to Jesus.
Close with a traditional prayer such as the Hail Mary or the Glory Be, then make the Sign of the Cross.

There it is — so simple, it's almost nothing at all. In the end, it's only making time each day to quietly look at Jesus. There are snares and difficulties along the way, but Saint Teresa would tell you to "let nothing steal your treasure." Life, she said, is "over in a couple of hours." It's like "a night at a bad inn." Jesus is forever. Jesus is worth anything and everything.

May St. Teresa of Jesus pray for us until we can say with her, "The Lord of Love is mine and I am truly his at last."

*Jesus * Mary * Elijah*

Acknowledgments

First and always, thanks to Joseph White and Mary Beth Giltner of OSV for seeing me and letting me write for you! Thank you to everyone who read the manuscript for me, made suggestions and observations, and gave encouragement: Fr. Gregory Ross, OCD; Fr. John McMannamon, SJ; Beth Ann Thibodeax; Gretchen Sams; my daughters, Maire and Roise Manning-Pauc (thanks, Roise, for reading the whole book aloud to me); Mark Hudgins; Kelly Brown; Molly Millroy; and Leticia Alba. Thanks to the Discalced Carmelite Community of St. Teresa Benedicta of the Cross and the Pontifical Biblical Institute of the Holy Hippie Sisterhood. And my parents for their support. Thank you to everyone on the Come to Mary's House Facebook page for encouraging me along the way as I posted about my progress.

And thank you, reader, for reading my little book. And to Saint Teresa herself, my gratitude for the matchless treasure she is, and to you, Lord, you, the beginning and end of all things, the Friend who we know loves us.

Books by St. Teresa of Ávila

Life (her autobiography)

The Way of Perfection

The Interior Castle

Foundations

About the Author

Shawn Chapman is the mother of two daughters, an enthusiastic grandmother of three children and a newborn. She is a caregiver, a committed vegan, and an avid reader. Shawn is a Discalced Secular Carmelite, the Catholic Columnist for Bryan-College Station Eagle Newspaper and author of *Come to Mary's House: Spending Time with Our Blessed Mother* (OSV). She lives in her native Texas with a gaggle of cats, dogs, chickens, and kids